moonsec

selected poems 1979–2007

Caeia March

'*A storyteller of great sensitivity.*'
– Spare Rib

'*A passionate writer, aware, alive and strong.*'
– Prime

'*Tantalising, sensual, slow-moving, tender and romantic.*'
– Gay Community News

*for Claire
from Caeia* xx
*With my warmest
wishes for all our
future collaboration
and creativity.*
October 2010

moonseanight

selected poems 1979–2007

Caeia March

PS AVALON
Glastonbury, England

First published in the U.K. in 2007 by PS Avalon

PS Avalon
Box 1865, Glastonbury
Somerset, BA6 8YR, U.K.
www.psavalon.com

Design: Will Parfitt

ISBN 978-0-9552786-3-1

Contents

Section One

Beyond a Limited Wedge of Sky

I think of the poems in section one in all their various forms, textures and rhythms as a selection of my "performance" poems. Many were presented in public in the nineteen eighties at venues throughout Britain, including mixed venues such as Peckham Community Arts Centre. I also read my work for the performance group 'Shooting Our Mouths Off', and with friends who belonged to The Worker Writers' Federation.

The title of this section is taken from my first published short story, A Limited Wedge of Sky, after I had left the children with their father during my coming out process in 1980.

Those were years of living in London, becoming sick with grief, which subsequently manifested as Chronic Fatigue in the aftermath of loss of the children, longing for wilderness and for an opportunity to heal all our wounds of separation.

Mark age Sixteen
Rob age Fourteen
Ten Minutes to Five
Amazons
Jacqueline du Pré

A Limited Wedge of Sky

Fear of square rooms
in a 1930's terrace.
Fear of my suburban
garden. Many years
it loves, to make a garden. I had watched
its edges
straight
-ening
me, one
hundred
feet long,
in   to
wifedom.
Closing
me in.
Separating
me   off
from
other
women.
I had planted   roses
              glimpsed
the   arching   rainbow
touch them   gently glowing
them into red   orange
yellow
in that
narrow
piece
of city
land.
Only a
limited
wedge
of sky

was
visible
to me
within
the
parallel
fences
of that
garden.

extract from short story, same title,
in *Everyday Matters 1* Sheba Feminist Publishers 1982

He Ran to School

He ran to school
clutching his first poem:

"If I was a flower, I would grow by the hour
and live merrily in the sun."

"If I was a leaf, I would be green, I would be new,
living until the autumn came,
and that's a long time, for a leaf."

Simple words, some rhyming
I helped him with his spellings –
He didn't talk at me
about spaceships   missiles
computers   or artillery.

And I wondered if there
might be some hope
for him
for us
if there is poetry
in his soul.

1979

Awakening

Awakening in a safe
dark bedroom   my ears
recorded   the surprise
of birdsong   and the
sleeping woman
beside me.

My arm was flung around
her shoulders   her warm
shape
folded to my belly, my thighs.

Shrill and happy
song birds heralded
morning's light horizon
like springtime ...

it was November.

November 1980

Ms World

Can you imagine
the howls of ridicule
jeers, hoots of contempt
as we stand there
she and I
on the glittering stage
her wearing the sash for Germany
and me for England?

We haven't got
the right shaped bottoms
neat and tight thirty-five inches
and Miss Germany's
breasts are too big
and Miss England's too small
to fit the thirty-six B that
every beauty queen must have.

Her waist is not slim
and my stomach
sags a little since I had two babies;
her legs are short and I have no ankles.
But ... just imagine
that her mouth smiles
inviting you inside
to allow you to know her.

Imagine if you can
her dark blue eyes
thick lashed full brimmed
with tears.

Know our quiet laughter
if you are near us
recognise us as we move
with wholeness
to the music
of our women only discos
free from male stares
and man-made images
of women's bodies.

Just imagine us singing
heads thrown back
our laughter loud now
in the September sunshine.
And think again
from whence
comes women's beauty.

October 1980

Published in *Dancing The Tightrope*, Women's Press 1987

Caer Caradoc

Last summer we tried a family holiday in Shropshire.
I tried to ignore the callings in me
of the women-loving women. I wanted
to stay with my little ones another nine years.
I claimed a day alone. I walked up to the highest
ledge of Caer Caradoc hill.
Blue and white sunlight. Full circle of sky.
Green valleys among the woman-rounded hills.
A field of thistles, seeds floating.
Red admiral butterflies fluttering above
the woman colours of purple and green.
Calm solitude reached into me. Nine years
is but minutes to the earth, so I decided I would
stay and mother my small sons.

At night their father and I
lay   along
the remote edges of our bed,
the valley between he and I wider then than the Ardèche,
where once we had camped in France.
We tried to span it with a sturdy bridge,
making each support and cable with our own hands,
talking all the time.
We thought it was possible
to each walk to the middle and live there,
but it wasn't a suitable place.

Some days I cannot let out the crying, if the swift image
of them the night I left appears at me out of October.
While my younger one released all the tension,
anguish, despair in body-shaking sobs,
my older son stood on the low bed
in the small spare room, so he was my height, and simply,
uncannily, put his arms around me, saying,
'I know Mummy, I know,' and kept his weeping

closed inside him.

Then, in this rented room, sleeping alone, I dream at night
of a future which has no colour: only white icebergs
splitting along the lines of their fractures. Intense
glacial dazzle – I never experienced white like this before.
Waking from this dream, my uterus
contracts in the rhythm of labour.
Pain reaches up inside me like a hand
pulling my children out of me.
My pillow and face are wet. I am howling
as do the animals who have their calves removed at birth.

Written 1981
Extract from *A Limited Wedge of Sky* op cit. 1982

Quantas Gallery : The art work of Ruth Faerber 1981

I knew when first I woke this morning
this would be a wise-woman day.
In the silent timelessness of this gallery
I am alone
here after hours
the gallery closed to all but me,
for this experience.

Ruth's reconstructed papers ranging
from one by two feet through six by seven
quietly assert strength and power,
like love,   if love is
compassion, connection, kindness.
Images   unworded   mould
concepts of time
here now then beyond
reach to me through
glass frames like breathing   out and in
there is no boundary
these messages flow linking
through space   across time-zones.

In Tasmania a woman hires
a paper-making mill,
her artist's hands pressing layering
choosing fixing selecting
envisioning
integrating pulp with leaves twigs
a feather some bark a fragment of cloth
some sand a sliver of stone
taking me home.

Years lost to human memory
geological time-traces buried
in the mind's silent recesses

like dried leaves whirled in fast spirals
into the cool dryness
of primeval caves there to rest
until discovered.

Bring to this gallery my questions
about time weave myself into this fabric
these questions into a labyrinth
follow my questions spiral and
swirl so curious yet so loved
so peaceful
absorb its white beige solitude
its grey blue heaven
a hint of indigo   a place
where writers and artists
understand one another
where writers have tables and spaces to think
to sleep, dream, form words from
these pictures this joyfulness
unlimited   at the beginning of all time.

I would choose never
to snatch time from its journey
in the busy-ness of days
nor to fail to find time
for the gentleness of calm wind on
the low slopes of a valley
nor catch only brief moments in the patterned
panic mindless manic turmoil
of my usual plans and schedules.

Here the artist knows my needs, nay, desire,
for time to just be
the artist layers my desires   includes them
feeds and nurtures them
grey-blue strata   feel the strength of
woman laughter

here it's possible to
breathe more slowly   here   in and out
in and out.

Beyond this art-space time-place
time costs money so I
must obey the rules made
for me by clocks bells buzzers
alarms watches telephones
so the seconds of my mind will speed
into minutes lost four hours yesterday
where did they go? why does it matter?
Losing time, killing time,
in too much hurry to find out
what else there is to learn.

Ruth's layers of history reveal
the ages of the earth
sand pebbles leaves a single twig
she comprehends that I, the viewer,
will engage with this longevity
I will slow down and be
I will absorb the messages
I will linger and love and trust
here breathing
in and out   in and out
slow the rhythm.

Scatterings of twigs
betokening fragments of lost
civilisations
feel the shimmering heat haze
over the desert
each grain of sand   moving   each molecule
of life giving oxygen   moving   I feel it all
so clearly now
a strand of feather grass.

Above the fury of the ocean   islands
- to the unknowing soul –
are but isolated forms of beauty
rising in primordial loneliness

but here   in this gallery
the illusion of separation
is shattered   islands rejoice
because they touch
beneath the surface
we are all part of everything.

The pulse that beats as its energy
opens a pine cone
moves also my own hand   held
pivoted on this table
my fingers move the pen forward
words from the centre of myself
music sounds around me
though the place is silent   empty.

Spirit of the papers in the frames
is my own spirit
fusion   the artist and the writer
blended feel it now
slow breath   in and out   in and out
my body leans forward towards the cicada
sitting coiled beneath the glass
on its bed of sand
natural colours surround me:
deep dark brown striations of the lowest foothills
white cream grey blue and veil of purple
shadow mauve   a hint of burgundy
my own memories easing into earth memories
have I been in these stratas before?
Each gathered pebble washed

a million waves ago
into its present position   each stone
shaped by boiling foaming waters.

My inner music shifts its intensity
its cadence
I hear times of disjuncture
disharmony discontinuity   recognition
that all is not forever peaceful
in the making of this planet.
Fury cracks stone
upon stone   screaming the schisms
breaking away
torrents taking time   tempests
flinging bones houses shacks and stones
birds animals people places
wide apart   across the
wind storm seas   the barren ravaged beaches.

Then once again the calm descends
the plenty bounty greenness
atonement for destruction.
Unquenchable the earth spirit unbreakable
the land sea moon tide solicitude.

On a clear warm night in the deserts
of Australia; stars out there in
a million galaxies
on the hills and valleys
and shores of England witness
from inside my own soul
we slow our tempo
with deliberate effort to listen to the earth
her tales of love and anger
challenge and confusion
tsunami and volcano
earthquake and tornado.

Then vision, as does the artist, the remaking
of this history, each fragment
respected, each molecule of humanity
in every place, with water
shelter food and clothing
connection culture community
with our own hands
re-creating.

First written in the Quantas gallery 1981. Re-written and edited
1990–2006 after visiting: Western Australia and the Pinnacles;
Oregon's Pacific coast which displays tsunami information and
warnings; and following the Indian Ocean/Indonesian tsunami of
26th December 2004, and the Kashmiri earthquake 2005.

Motherwords

At last we talk   a beginning, perhaps.
You, a mother by choice
erotic woman,   understanding   so well
the bond of sensuous joy
that links you to your girl child.

Listening, I hear you with some pain, however,
for there cannot be with my sons that same resonance
there remains a chasm
not of their making
not of my choosing
as they reach   and I reach   across
to touch fingers   trying to   span the gap
succeeding   now and then   holding   laughing.

I think of you   and your daughter
sometimes as I soap my sons   in their bath
splashing water   singing   playing bubbles.

I think of you and her   me and them   and dream
a future   that includes us all.

1982-4

Myself age Thirteen

Young girl
fluey cold
high bed
picks up
old ted

dreams whirl
palms hold
old ted's
fontanel
bald head

womb curl
wants own
child's head
sometime
in bed

young girl
dream sown
in bed
secret wish
instead

dreams whirl
her own
son's head
fontanel
high bed

womb curl
grow up
instead
don't tell
old ted

The Wanting

Young woman
with-it   reads science news
how to make boy babies
how fast sperms swim   where eggs are.
Taking temperatures   scheming ovulation
wanting a pregnancy   whole of my body
every cell yearned   longed in anticipation
to be pregnant   intense searing wanting
red hot chilli peppers wanting
child child child
was it biological psychological meterological sociological
astrological geological –
what kind of earth science put me there then wanting?
wanting wanting wanting
to be full with child   carrying a child
bun in the oven up the duff in the club
when it happened
that first time   my skin glowed
my hair thickened   my body responded
with yes yes yes

looking back   to age thirteen
I know the event   when it all began
that wanting   wanting wanting
in bed with a cold   I held an old hard-headed bear
shaven and decrepit   from my cousin
ten years my senior
by chance   cradled that bear   my womb turned over   that
first ever womb-lurch
all alone   no one near me
virgin till I married   wanting

I knew the exact moment I got pregnant
please don't ask me how I knew
I just knew   no science to it
I don't know how
we women know such things

2007

A Message to the Collective

I would like to go
to a meeting where my voice
is heard
and talk about my
struggles to become a lesbian writer.

I had two babies over ten years ago.

I would like to know you to let you near enough to listen
to my talking, my joys, or speaking bitterness.

I had two babies over ten years

Those of you who say I had a choice.
You with no childcare. Talking fast
at me with your explanations.
Mothers are well trained to listen.

I had two babies over

You want me to hear you,
don't you? You have stories to tell
of your lives. I have time.

I had two babies

You talk about your struggles
how to gather your thoughts together
your ideas, the colours in your minds.
You move as quickly as you dare through
the boring items on the agenda. Not terribly
interested you say in

I had two

organising childcare. Much more
fascinated if I move on to discuss
the techniques of short story writing

I had

and the content and form of
political fiction, poetry.

I

I have to go now because
my children are waiting.

First published in Christian McEwen ed: *Naming The Waves*
Virago 1988

Contradictions

Now I call myself a dyke
stand on flat sand
toes in the ocean
arms raised to the sky
the silver moonseanight
in front of me
and I am less afraid
but where are my children
and how do I name them?

I name them as my contradictions
which I claim and face and love.
I name them as mine
though I left them with their father.

They know who I am
and how and when to name me.

They know that I love them
and that where they are concerned
my survival and theirs
depends on the honesty
with which I dare to say
that this part of my boundary
is blurred.

They may grow up to be gay or straight
but I am their mother
a woman
and they can never
grow up to be women.

Neither of them has made this society
in which they were birthed
from out of my body

and if they are to survive
they must like themselves
and love themselves
for there are enough of them already
who live by hate.

1983-4

First published in *Writing as a Lesbian Mother* in In Other
Words – Writing as a Feminist ed. Gail Chester and Sigrid
Nielson, Hutchinson1987

You are not ….

a real lesbian
>   you once were married

a real separatist
>   you love those boys

a real feminist
>   you wanted sons

a real mother
>   you're just part-time

Extract adapted from *Writing as a Lesbian Mother* in In Other
Words – Writing as a Feminist ed Gail Chester and Sigrid
Nielson, Hutchinson1987

Mark age Sixteen

Life was my gift to you, all those years ago.
A life for you, born out of me.
I'm glad for you to have your life to live.
It's yours not mine. I don't want control over it.
It's yours to take control of as you wish.

You are passionate, philosophical: deep possibility
inside you of fulfilment and loving. There is ample time
ahead. You seem to know that already.
You owe me nothing of course. When I am old,
I want you to feel that I set you free
from obligations to me.
You do not need my approval for your decisions. I feel
intuitively that many will be wise ones.
That doesn't mean your life will be without mistakes: you are
human like me - and my life is full of mistakes.
But make no mistake about it,
you weren't one of them. You were one of the
best things I ever did.

I didn't know at your age what possibilities
there were for me.
Becoming who I am wasn't simple. I had to search
in uncharted waters, capsized a few boats on the way.
All I need to know now is you wouldn't vote
for laws that would make my life harder. Not that I
expected an easy life.
But my life is very joyful. Full of loving, wonderful
people.
You being one of them.

1988

Rob age Fourteen

You've just started growing to the sky.
Turn around by next birthday, we'll be
eye to eye.
One day I'll be down here
five foot three –
you'll be towering over me.

But I shall still have an image of you
in a fun-fur cowboy waist-coat,
with a shocking pink
felt hat, worn all day
so the ladies couldn't stroke
your white blond curls.
You took it off only to sleep
placing it by your feet
with big Ted and blue mouse.

I'll still see that cheeky grin
and crooked tooth, where a wall
and your bike
had a fight.

You've just started growing to the sky.
Such a lean, lively body –
I watch you, laughing,
used to wear you straddled on my hip:
bonded from birth, I always adored you.
From the day
you learned to speak, you stopped
just like me, only to sleep.
I shine, listening to your stories –
no pause button - except in the library.
I studied there, with you beside me:
you would be silent, then,
near me, happy with jigsaws,

an hour, you amazed me.

I picture you on traction, in hospital,
tried not to cry in front of you
wondered if you'd ever learn
to walk again.
When you come home, I said, we'll have
a party for you, with candles.
Instantly: Can I have four?
Then next birthday I can have five
and catch up with Mark.

If I start down memory lane
I'll be travelling forever
better stay in the present
where we love and miss
one another.

1988

Ten minutes to Five

The afternoon's work is almost done -
my table neatly rectangled
with pages of prose   narratives
letters diaries poems.

My head focuses on the
seventeenth century   life and times
of the people of London.

All in a day's labour: the process
of the working writer
my books lie open   words
lined up   sequenced into
sorrows joys lies and truth.

But separately from me
with a life, it seems, of their own
beyond the creative discipline
of these minutes
and this hour
my breasts   alive and wanting
await your return.

1987

Amazons

Mother of small Black daughters,
I the mother of tall white sons
salute you.

Riding my night-winged horse
left breast removed
quiver of arrows slung
across my right shoulder
I leap the raging rivers
between us.

Horses' hooves clattering sparks
wording the wide warm plains
paper forest fantasies
to rest in.

Little women, we are warriors, both.

1986-7

Jacqueline du Pré

Her love of life and music danced
from the hem of her long skirt
to the pads on her finger tips –
her hands arms wrists fluid moving
like ballet her head and shoulders
swaying this way and that –
her whole body encircling her cello.

Sadness and intensity flowed through me.
Elgar's cello concerto took on new meanings
as we watched the woman on the television
performing. She loved being alive,
being in love, being music.

They were telling us that she had died.
Forty two. A few months older than me.

Three of us were in the room. Our cat, who
loves us, picked up on our feelings,
came rubbing around, offering herself.

On the floor, my lover, sitting legs splayed,
took the cat to her. Together they swayed
as the animal stretched, fur belly exposed,
cello-like, being played, playing.
A sense of urgency enclosed me –
I crept closer to them both, drinking the
sounds, breathing the music.
Jacqueline was laughing – each cell
of her body from toes to strands of hair,
was alive, moving,
giving, reaching, challenging.

I want to pour out joy like Jacqueline
filling the rest of my time, earth-time,
like she did, making something for
others to treasure, after I'm gone,
like she did.

November - December 1987

Section Two

Cornwall

In September 1988 I was diagnosed with Chronic Fatigue Syndrome, a diagnosis made by my GP, a diagnosis which gave me an explanation and insight into what was happening to my body. I subsequently edited a book of writings by women with ME, as it was then known. My then partner Keri Woods and I decided to leave London for the West Country, and my sons, who lived with their father, were absolutely wonderful about that relocation.

'Just go for it Mum,' said Mark, 'You'll get well again there.' Rob said, 'I can just see you in old green wellies, Mum, stomping around your garden.'

My move to Cornwall had been longed for since the summer of 1985, on my first visit to Brisons Veor, a house on the very end of Cape Cornwall in which women writers, musicians and artists could take a respite and do their creative work. I lived in Cornwall part time from 1988 and then full time until 1998. Keri and I separated in 1992, and we are still good friends.

Cape Cornwall 1985   *Jewels*
                         Dance
                         Ledges
                         Brisons Veor - The Fantasy

Cot Valley in December
Clarification
Friend
Dance of Bones
The Song of Iseult
The Ice Plants

Jewels

Sunlight showers sharp
glass droplets on blue water.
Wind drives crystals to
Porth Ledden's cove.
Has time cast her net
beyond the indigo horizon
while I slept,
trawled the Aegean,
returned on the dawn tide
with this Greek island?

Dance

Like blue lurex, the ocean moves
in the humid afternoon:
a silver-threaded dancer
laughing in the sun
timing her body
to her own rhythm
while the rocks strum a deep
bass undertone
reverberating
from the dancer's floor.

Ledges

Window ledges: a jug of blossoms
red and white scented williams
bowl of plums   deep crimson
waiting for ripening;

cliff ledges: thrilling, enticing,
alluring, inviting, softened by fluffy figs
defiantly hanging through wind and storm;

sea ledges: rocks waiting to become sand
waves dripping levels turning tides
seals playing, diving, creating balance
from danger, courting the currents,
owning the edges.

I move like them between the layers of
our relationship, charting the patterns,
the familiar insecurities ... were it not
for you, here, now, this place
might be a precipice of loneliness,
the unknown terrifying, the gales hostile,
the enveloping mist, a shroud.

Brisons Veor: the fantasy

I'd like a barn, a large hairy dog, four rabbits,
and several goats, two cats, one tortoise;
an oak tree planted near the barn to grow into
maturity with me
flowers beside and around the barn,
a quiet place for thee and me: we
could sit in the sun and stay indoors
by an open fire when the west winds howl.

I'd like a sunny loft in which to write
to ride my bicycle along the coast path
walk and walk as the sun sinks
over the ocean.

I'd like friends to visit, a lover to love me,
solitude plenty. My sons to come for holidays
bring their partners, bring their friends,
bring their children, see the place,
the animals, the countryside,
and a lover to be loved by me.

Cot Valley in December

Trees bend low under lichens, palest green edged white
and bright orange fungi lighten the undergrowth like
unexpected solstice candles.

I am listening to the everlasting water pouring along
its track of stones rocks pebbles: each sound a natural
instrument supernatural orchestra   water on stone
wind in wood.

Beech nuts that have sprung six seven feet high
are leafless now, dark brown stems and flaming
pink brown tops, twigs like squirrel tails jumping
to the sky. White bark backcloths are stunted birches
while the river rattles on like dried seeds in an old
wooden drum

to the edge of the world where the waters have salt
and fish; the wind whips vinegar in my face;
and the child in me remembers Yorkshire.

1987

Clarification

Cot Valley waters washed my mind
clean and clear of all confusions.
I was the tumbling river, winter's weight
inside me, going home.
I was the weathered rocks facing westwards
waiting for trouble.
I was the green moss clinging there
growing in danger round and soft.
I was the breaker each and every wave
urgently crashing, retreating in tatters
gathering myself up for the next time
the next and the next.
I was the pathway back inland
anchored despite meanderings,
capable of bringing myself to myself
to my own door, over my own threshold,
keeping myself safe.

1987

Friend

Friend   I want to be there with you
starting a new life
living far away from
city rules traffic fumes high rise noise cries
there where the moon pours silver energy
from the sun   other side of night
down onto land and ocean
there   where
waves of black mirror silver are
splintering on Cornish headlands
while the women
in the tea shop   read poetry
each to the other
slowing down
time to notice that the moon has more
sky to swim in.

Friend   I want to be there with you.

1987

Dance of Bones

Between the worlds two women
sleep. Dreaming into one another's dreaming.
Dream   Image   Imagine.
More women enter.   Who are they?
Are they real? Are they spirit? They join hands
begin to swirl   on sacred grass   a ring of stones.
They dance   they dance   a dance of bones.
Where are they now? Dans Maen – The Dancing Stones.
Nineteen maidens in a trance, turned to stone
they dared   they dared to dance.

Sacred grass   a ring of stones
how is   this serpent dance of bones?
The figures turn and swing around
a ritual dance on hallowed ground
a swirling serpent dance of night.
In the sky a thin-armed moon
silver sliver in the dome
cradling a hidden shadow egg
dark egg   dark shell   a shadow shape
which holds inside its shell the tunes
and all the words you ever need
a serpent song   a crescent arm
they dance   they dance   the crescent moon.

Moon is a serpent snake in the dome
the women dance   they dance around
snaking the moon upon the ground
they dance   they dance   a dream   a trance
a serpent dance   a thin-armed moon
who holds the shape   the shadow shape
a cosmic egg   a womb   an eye
image held in the dome of the sky
for ancient peoples used to know
how the serpent moon would grow

and dance her there with ritual sound
weaving themselves on hallowed ground
dancing a serpent crescent moon
dancing   the eggsnakewombeye tune.

Snake was the thin-armed moon in the sky
reflected from the sun at noon
and underground   as spring and river
the rainbow serpent flowed for ever
with thread and blood and womb and loom
snake was the earth and mirrored moon
when all was woman womb and tune.

Egg was the symbol, shadow and dark
holding the secrets of fire and spark
with tune and words and women wise
in the dome of the sky   when the moon was new
their feet they danced and sang and flew
above the grass   between the stones
they danced   they danced   the dance of bones.

Inside the egg inside the skull
were written all the words of wise
at night in the dark   in the thin-armed moon
holding the secrets of blood and tune
when music flowed between the stones
they danced   they danced   the dance of bones.

Slip through time and land and sky
between the worlds   inside the womb
to feel the pulse of woman tune
the words are old   before the stones
when people knew the dance of bones.

When women loved women
and the earth was young
then female was the sacred one

snake was sacred and the old were wise
the shadow egg was the mother's eyes and
blood was red and good and clean
and thread was loom and snake and flow
when people watched the new moon grow
reflecting all the noontide light
they sang and drummed and tapped their feet and
snaked the moon between the stones and
danced   they danced   the dance of bones.

There was no rape   no father-right   no child
afraid to sleep at night   no girl to scorn
nor vilify   nor call her witch   nor evil eye
no wife to beat   nor child to sell   no girl
to bed against her will   when woman was moon
and earth and sun   and female was the sacred one
then people danced on ritual ground   and twirled
and sang and spun around   around the stones
to the heartbeat drum   spirals woven
under the moon
and feet they flew   above the stones
as people danced the dance of bones.

The names of the mother were many and all
when people heard the full moon call
some are written and some forgotten and
some arc lost and some are torn and
some are burned and some are raped
and some are whipped around a stake
through the hearts of women broken
some are gone and some are spoken
some are harassed and vilified and
some are tortured and denied
some are hidden, some rewritten and
some are being rediscovered
danced and tuned and newly worded
loved and hummed and re-recorded.

Know the names and know the call
know the names of one and all
all the mothers all the daughters
all the girls and all the babies
not forgotten lost in bones
when we spiral dance the dancing stones.

Under the noon and under the sky under
the moon thin-armed and silver   know the serpent
know the call   know the rivers freely flowing
know the blood the new moon growing
know the woman's womb exploring
know the woman's mind recording
know the bodies dreaming loving.

Open the book the new words making
open the night the dream time taking
careful lovers bodies flowing women lovers
bodies knowing   words from the moon
night time defining
words from the egg   the patterns shining
words from the womb the new words daring
lesbian wisdom bodies sharing.

The dragon women are living growing
the dragon breath is the serpent showing that
the garden of Eden was not the first
the earth was there before the worst   tales
were told about Eve's evil   the dragon breath
will rise and rise   she will not stay
where the men dismissed her   she won't obey
the rules of them   who kill   and burn   and tell their lies.

The women watch and dance the moon and
again they learn the oldest tunes and
bones that once were turned to stone are

living now and newly grown
so serpent-woman sheds her skins
she reads the words and then begins
to dance   and dance   with loved ones
knowing she once more can make the tune
they danced   they danced   beneath the moon.

*Dans Maen – The Dancing Stones is the Cornish name for the Merry Maidens stone circle

*First published in *Reflections* - my fourth novel - based in Cornwall on the legend of Tristan and Iseult. The entire novel was written as cycles of sounds, without chapters, entirely in rhythm. Published by The Women's Press 1995

The Song of Iseult

I am the green of grass the red of flame the blue of water
the yellow of bone. The orange of sunlight the purple of ling
the indigo of moonlight on the old quartz stone.
I am the green of heathland the red of tongue
the blue of egg the yellow of gorse. The orange of rose-hip
the purple of sage the indigo of shadow in the season's turn.
I am woman and serpent one and the same; I am dragon
and sunlight the sky and the moon.
I am your lover naked in the afternoon.
I am the earth and nature egg and bird; I am the song
and singer the dancing word.
I sleep now curled but watch me in the morning. I am
woman and earth. You have had your warning.
I am peaceful in the old times, polluted in the new.
I shall pour my acid rain on you.
I am healing and hurting one and the same. I am old
I am young and I cannot be tamed.

Extract from The Song of Iseult, in *Reflections*, The Women's Press 1995

The Ice Plants*

We watched for weeks as they died back
into the ground : long unsightly sickly
stems, frostbitten.
Today we saw they'd begun again,
brave pale leaves, round rosettes, preparing.
Inside we're as cold as they are, in hostile soil.
We would appreciate some summer sunshine.

It was a wonderful midwinter season, this year.
Mark and Rob, tall and gentle, relaxed and loving.
Us two lovers and three women friends.
Presents and party hats. Greenwich Park at sunset,
the winter sky deepening over London - lights
going on across the Thames, the Isle of Dogs,
beyond that, Walthamstow, my lover's home.*

Over Xmas dinner we kidded, pulling crackers:
What's the difference between a cat and a comma?
I dunno Mum: What is the difference between a cat and a
comma?
A cat's got claws at the end of its paws,
and a comma's a pause at the end of a clause!!
Groans, winks, pull-the-other-ones.

Now – a pause – imposed silence on me and my writing:
Clause 14 became Clause 27 became Clause 28.

Surely you didn't expect your kind of books to be
in libraries, dear? Mum's voiced chilled me –
ice cubes down my phone wire,
clattering out the ear piece into a New Year drink.

New Year round an open fire in a farm in Cornwall.
End of the land. End of a year in which
Three Ply Yarn* did enter libraries, I did receive

letters from Devon to Dundee.
I grew green and strong. Voiced.

Cornwall. Wet, wild and windy. Ghostly in its clinging,
mysterious beauty. Two days the mists lifted, we saw
beyond the sunset horizon, glimpses of freedom.

On other days the rain held us in its peace.
Indoors editing eighty thousand words, couldn't take
a holiday from The Hide and Seek Files,* but
time zones are different in Cornwall –
the land reaches behind the dolmens, bringing extra
minutes forward, from Neolithic peoples
on forgotten moor-lands.

Moonseanight. Sea wind and rain held no
respect for dark or light.
We drifted into thirty-six hour days, wrote many
a new clause those magic moments.

London again, scheduled editing again.
Clock-time : day and night routines:
dedication to the craft: survival with discipline:
a certain weary determination
to birth a few green buds from tired rootstocks.

Then, as if by magic, words whizz around
our networks. Meet on Saturday, our first Olga*
Saturday. Imperial War Museum.

Twelve thousand gather, in the park.
Like Emperor penguins we bunch,
hunched against Antarctic chill.
We huddle and we sing, fringed by winter's
leafless enormous trees, waiting with us
in that cold park, waiting and hoping,
for the greening of spring.

Not a cat to be seen in the park. Indoors, under
buildings, seeking shelter. One or two folk have dogs.
Some folk have wheels, are seated among us.
Suddenly, through glimpses of side streets,
we see – huge horses –
with massive imposing horsemen in
Darth Vader helmets – riders with riot shields –
their steeds trained to step broadside
into demos, into us.
Organic sound – collective gasp:
We are surrounded. We are trapped. How do
you confront a police horse
from a wheelchair?

Frosted feet, scarf wrapped faces, our breath
steaming, human beings
chilled to the bone, freezing cold,
wanting freedom.
Places for our books in the libraries.
Stories to tell, no where to tell them.
Voices to speak, no where to let them rest.
Restless wind my voice becomes, searching for echo.

Speaker after speaker with megaphones.
Call and response. Are we giving in: No.
Are we going back in the closet: No.
Our chant begins, around and around the frozen air:
for love and for life we are not going back.
for love and for life we are not going back.

Then later, advice from our organisers:
we ask you to leave in fives, in tens,
please no pushing, please, no panic.
Link your arms, walk very slowly,
don't let go of your children, or your friends.
A whisper among us, stay together – don't get picked off –
remember the quota of arrests for their records,

they must maintain their stats.
Two strangers arrested – for kissing by the park gates.
For kissing. Arrested. Truly. We witness.

We pause, the week after the demo,
hold in our death-knell feelings of despair,
when our surroundings have turned against us,
so very, very cold.
Try to stay focussed, try to be confident,
watch our ice plants in our frozen front garden
gather together their tiny spurts of energy.
They push and push undeterred,
time-lapsed, like slowed-down nature films.

Holding one another, we call our loved ones:
we are a real family, aren't we?
My children, my lover, my sister, her
children, her husband: who is there
to say we are pretending?

Remember that Christmas cracker: what's the difference
between a cat and a comma?
Well, beware my claws at the end of this pause:
for love and for life, we are not going back.
for love and for life, we are not going back.

---

* Following Clause 28, The Ice Plants was performed at many venues
throughout Britain.
* My lover at that time was Keri Woods and is still a dear friend.
* *Three Ply Yarn*, my first novel, was published in 1986 and selected for
Feminist Book Fortnight 1987
* *The Hide and Seek Files*, was published in 1988.
* Olga - Organisation for Lesbian and Gay Action
* Saturday, January 9th 1988

Section Three

The Ballad of Ellan Vannin

Ellan Vannin is the Gaelic name for the Isle of Man where I was born. In my fifth novel it is also the fictional name for a Manx witch – a healer and wise woman from the thirteenth century whose child dies of a cot death, for which she is blamed, and killed.

Tarnagh Callister, nicknamed Tarn, is a fictional character from the late twentieth century who lives in Penzance, but was born in the Isle of Man, where she lived until she was fifteen, at which time her family moved because her father went to work for the Cable and Wireless Company in Porthcurno. Her family name, Callister, comes from both her maternal and paternal ancestry, because her parents were two Manx cousins who married. Her heritage is a combination of fiction and fact – the name Callister being my own maternal grandmother's heritage on the island. When Tarn's grandchild dies whilst in her care, the ultimate terror for any grandparent, she returns to her birthplace, renting a small wooden cabin in the hills. It is there that she meets the ancestral healer, Ellan Vannin.

The ballad was created by me during a period of my own grief and healing, during a time of major upheaval in a lesbian relationship, which began in 1992 and from which I subsequently escaped in 1998, to my very great relief. The strength to leave that relationship remains with me and sustains me to this day in my long term happiness and trust with my present lover, friend and life partner, Cynth Morris.
As a novelist I draw on all of life's experience for my fiction and eventually I wove parts of Tarn's story into the fifth novel entitled *Between the Worlds*. Parts of the Ballad of Ellan Vannin were set to music in the late nineties.

Glossary

Tramman tree - elder tree
Carranes - sandals with leather thongs tied around the ankles.
Keeill - small church or chapel, sometimes a remote hermitage.
Kelly - a family name found very frequently in the island.
Magistrate - in nineteenth century folk songs or ballads this would
have been deemster but for the thirteenth century I chose to keep the
more familiar term - magistrate.
Corkhill - a Manx surname.
Vorrie, Greba - Manx female first names.
Spellings for mythological figures and folk figures have been taken
from the standard (chosen) spellings used in the Manx Museum
reference section, Douglas, Isle of Man. If they are self explanatory in
the ballad, they aren't needed in this glossary.
See of Rome - the Vatican, the Pope's closest associates.
Slieu Whallion or Slieuwhallion - a hill about two miles from Peel
opposite the Tynwald Mount.

History

1258 is the exact year during the Thirteenth Century when I have
placed this story. This is just before the end of the period of the
Norse-Manx Kings. Subsequently, in 1265, Norway gave the island
to Scotland. 'Scotland and Norway then disputed the ownership of
the Isle of Man until 1333, when Edward III granted the island under
feudal rights to the first Earl of Salisbury'. The island has always had its
own separate parliament, the Tynwald, derived from the Norse system
called 'Thing' and continues to remain independent of Westminster
with no representation there. Constitutionally, the Isle of Man now
operates as a Crown Dependency, with a Governor-General. This
information and quote is from Robinson and McCarroll, *The Isle of
Man, Celebrating a Sense of Place*, Liverpool University Press, 1990.

The Ballad of Ellan Vannin

I.

Listen to the ocean, the ocean, the ocean,
early morning tide, slow surging washing clean.
Listen to the ocean, the ocean, the ocean,
sunlight on the low waves; listen to us speak.

Calm tide and sea birds calling, calling, calling,
listen to our voices - your heart longs for peace.
Listen to the wise ones, the wise ones, the wise ones
calling, calling, calling you now.

Your birthplace was our island, a stormy place, a violent place:
your birthing was a trial of strength, a journey
tight with pain. You arrived here naked, blood-soaked
and screaming: we call you to come back to us,
sometime soon again.
You didn't have a soft birth, a gentle time, a warm time,
nor have you had a soft life, an easy life, a safe life:
a birthing so violent a thunder and a lightning –
a girl child, Tarnagh, daughter of the storm,
you are not calm nor still nor sweet, nor are you quiet at dawn.
Aptly named, you know this now: a Gaelic thunderstorm.

Of the line of Callister, born on little island,
the line of Callister - we foremothers knew –
farming folk and moor-land folk
our strength is with you still.

Listen to the ocean, the ocean, the ocean,
listen to the women of your line reaching you:
back into the moor-lands, the hill farms, the
cliff walks, there on little island, our voices call
to you.

Tarnagh of thunder, we call to you, we call to you:
we have on little island a ballad to unfold –
skim along the cloud ridge, fly to little island,
listen to your forebears: our song is very old.

Here is one who calls you, calls you, calls you –
later than the Vikings from the era of The Pope.
Sing this song of thunder, of women and of terror,
sing this song of healing love and never give up hope.

This is not a simple song, the words are strange, a tale untold,
the story of one woman - her voice as yet unknown.
Sing this to the ocean and sing it to the earth;
you were the girl child - the one from little island
from the line of Callister, the line of your birth.

Tarnagh not a simple name, a calm name, a silent name -
we have named you *thunder*, the daughter of the storm.
Do not fear to know us – our love is with you still
there's a tempest on the island around the witches' hill.

Speak your name of thunder, of thunder, of thunder -
speak the scream that surges across the gentle lake.
Tarn is a still place, a quiet place, a slow place;
Tarnagh is an old name, a wise name, a strong name.
When women speak with thunder, the earth must shake,
still waters break and songs must flow and ballads
grow from hidden depths the truth to make.

Listen to the ocean, the ocean, the ocean –
we sing to you your heritage, a ballad from the soul –
do not dread these hidden words, our voices, nor our call;
Sing this song of thunder, of women and of terror,
sing this song of love and trust, then learn to name us all.

Listen to the ocean, the ocean, the ocean –
listen to the women of your line reaching you.

We sing to you your heritage - a ballad of the soul
come to little island: an early morning call.

II.

Cur failt erriu gys Ellan Vannin.
Soft female voice, our air stewardess
welcomes us, as the wheels touch down.
Mona's Isle. The land of my foremothers.

What are my expectations? I have none as I
stand, reach to the overhead locker for my
hand luggage and move slowly with the other
passengers along the gangway to the exit.

The cabin door is open, the steps in position:
I am on the metal platform, about to place
my left foot down onto the first step when
I am greeted in the old traditional manner,
by my grandmother's grandmother.

It happens each and every time. And each time
I don't expect it to happen again,
though maybe I should, by now.

There are warm hands, very lightweight, placing
an invisible hand-knitted shawl, with a thick
hand-knotted fringe around my shoulders.
There are no words. There is no voice. No one
else has seen or heard or felt a thing.
But I am being smiled upon, and this I know:
she is my grandmother's grandmother
on my mother's side, of the line of Callister
and she wants me here home, on our island, again.

The shawl will remain with me while I am here.
She will not come to me with words or presence

though I will be comforted by the shawl and it holds
her kind messages of love and continuity.
I am known. I am loved. I am wanted here.

I catch the bus into town, observing the rolling
fields and wooded lanes absorbing once again
the rise and fall of the intonation. A sing-song version
of the English language is spinning through the air.

Satisfied, I lean back and listen. Our bus crosses
safely over The Fairy Bridge, so perhaps
other passengers are, like me, acknowledging
the little people by paying silent respects.
My shawl is warm, silent, invisible like Mannanan's
cloak. My grandmother's grandmother stayed behind
near the airport.
As for me, I am home.

III.

You came in the night. Warm comfort.
Here on little island, by the moor-land's edge.
You have green eyes and dark brown hair –
I know who you are and watch you there. They ask me often the
story of my name;
I say it is Gaelic. My mother was Manx.
A Celt, from little island,
my name has many meanings.
Softly they say it, softly and call me Tarn.
But I am not soft, nor quiet at dawn –
my full name is Tarnagh, child of a storm.
Of thunder and lightning was I born
of fire and earth and moving rivers
of lakes and streams and glens and faeries
glaciers cool and deep earth magma.

And you? I see you spinning there,

you know me by my name:
Tarnagh child of a mountain storm
of turbulent seas in the month of June.
We share an island, you and I – your name is
Ellan Vannin.

Ellan Vannin come to me. I invite you,
I invoke you: you are knowledge,
being, presence. You're the
cunning woman, the herbalist, she who
has waited for me to arrive
in this ancestral place – to respond to you,
to find your strength, to learn to heal.
You turn to observe me, your eyes are kind
and your name is Ellan Vannin.

You bring dark secrets, old legends.
Your knowledge spans the centuries
between us : beautiful, tranquil eyes that care –
there by the fire, which sparks and crackles,
in this, the early morning.
So I speak your name, perhaps not aloud.
Who knows? You do. You know my voice,
inside, outside, you are understanding me
and grandmother's grandmother's shawl
is soft around my shoulders.
I arrived here naked, bloody and screaming
and I know I have been here before.
The light was fading: I unlocked this door
on the edge of the green sea-moor.

Safer than a sea-scape this moor
is enclosed so the infinity of the mist
is an illusion: eternity is not forever
but shape-shifts back into valleys and hills
holding this house on the edge of never.
Today from the window the tidal mist

ebbs and flows enclosing my house
on a greengrass beach
fringed by a green-topped hedge:
until the tide turns, the mist, retreating,
now rolling back its own horizon,
reveals fields and woods, held in the bowl
of the distant hills, contented and contained.

In the manner of the wise ones,
I stand beneath the tramman tree,
turning myself inside out,
opening my heart to the healing.

IV.

Rain beats against the house, sharp pins
tapping the windows. You didn't have glass,
just shutters of heavy sacking to protect you
from the wind. They did not protect you
from the people.

I saw you in the green garden at sunset,
raising your arms to Bride, the mother,
she who became Saint Bridget.
You knelt, placing
your palms on the small boulder
under the tramman tree. Then I recognised
the place where you buried your baby.

You're solid, your body rocking
to and fro, your hands on the stone, your lips
murmuring. You're not crying –
you are praying. You don't hold with
the new ways,
will not worship in the keeill,
no matter how simple its
sturdy stone building,

set low in the heather.
Those are not your Gods, nor ever
will be. So it concerns you not
that the priests and elders rejected
you and your baby, since you adhere not
to their beliefs.

What is it to you if their priests
belong to the kingdom of Man and The Isles
blessed by the Bishop of Norway or if he,
in his turn, is sanctified by the See of Rome.
But your heart aches for the child who died
and your soul longs for freedom from blame.

I know so much more about you every day:
how you lived here alone - how people
abused you, name-called you, when your child
stopped breathing in her crib.
A wooden crib with small rockers,
handed down from your mother.
Ellan, I watch you
picking up the small cold body,
rocking her in your arms, willing
breath into her.
You wrap her inside your shawl, cradle her
for hours by the fire. They find you there,
rocking, keening, and point the finger
because you live alone.

Morning – the post van comes.
A letter from my daughter.
Blaming me. Blaming me. Isn't going
to forgive me. Has given up her job, sold
her flat, is returning to the husband
who beat her.
I observed that she could,
always dreaded that she would.

I am here now, also alone, witnessing
the ebb and flow of cloud and rain
in the valley; learning that
a local poet has called these hills
his great ships on the sky-line – they come
full-sailing blue-black
when the midnight sky begins to clear.
Is this an inland sea, this valley of mist and
moving rain? Its waters cry down, gather
to the river, dissolve, return to the coast.
So you see, Ellan Vannin, why we are here,
the two of us, you and I, each alone
each in her own grief. Reaching out, with
resolute courage: I replied to your voice.
Stepping forward, every moment is just
past, every moment is just now,
every moment is just future.
Moment by moment, that's
what wisdom means, nay, demands,
traversing the healing bridge.

V.

Washed. Everything fresh blowing dry in
the wind. Blue-grey clouds and turquoise streaks
on a sharply defined sky-line.
Charcoal rope-line drawn along the horizon so
the hills don't billow up into the sky: hills held
solid against the ground, pegged down like huge green
tents, summits at the ridge poles, middles sagging.

Near to the little wooden house dark ivy stars
gleam, brushed and patted into shape
like nineteen-fifties hair-dos. Wet bars on the veranda
black in silhouette against the morning light.

The morning opens to the day: I open myself
to you, Ellan Vannin. Here in this wooden house
with a ribbon washing line, after night rain, hung with
glass beads, not one missing. One solitary pigeon
sits on a single brown post, taking stock of the
unhurried vegetable plot, where lime-green grass
is so wet you couldn't step without sinking.

But the rain is merely a memory. You wouldn't think
that the night was wild, the wet wind lashing
our water-whip seas. Oh Ellan Vannin, this
would be a fearsome place without you – and I
have been a lifetime travelling here.

I move to the window to absorb the scenery,
to allow slow time to seep into my soul.
Those distant hills are you, green witch,
reclining, heavy with the past,
pregnant with the future. Here, in the present
they just are. Like me. I am. I am being here.
My name for home is: Ellan Vannin.
The wooden house is an ark in a storm;
a strong wooden boat; the dove holds an
olive branch in her mouth.
Land is in sight.

Insight. My daughter's letter must
not destroy me. Maybe there will be others
while she searches in vain for
a route through this tragedy.
Vorrie. Granddaughter. Small. Smiling. Huge wide
vulnerable eyes. Curly arms and legs.
Vorrie. Child of the line of Callister.
Grandchild. She was a grand little wee little
one. She was. Was. Was.
Yes, she was.

The university people
are studying all the cases of babies
who have, like baby Vorrie, simply, silently,
stopped breathing.   They will
find the answers.   Let them please
find the answers.   For your sake,
and mine, Ellan Vannin.
Now with your help, I will summon
all my courage, for your sake
if not my own.

Did you ask yourself, night after sleepless night
what more you could have done? Did you
look out at bleak morning's high moor-lands
Ellan Vannin, wanting someone's
encircling arms? With your heart filled by grief
did you reach out to Greba Kelly?
Were you awed by your mutual need
those snatched and clandestine
mornings?

The only other who understands
me (apart from you who called me
here) the only one who knows
from the inside,
because it happened to *her* daughter too,
is Gwen Corkhill, who will come tomorrow,
so tomorrow can't come soon enough,
for me.

Gwen and Tarn, childhood friends,
little girls following the faeries
in Groudle glen, sunlit by celandines.
Dancing dappled delighted
under canopies, choreographing bold ballets
beside a tumbling river,
then running, to emerge through

childhood's sublime sunshine,
to the pebbles,
where water rattles hard to the sea.
Holding hands, skimming stones, not a care
in the world, we romanced growing up,
having babies. We wanted girls, two each,
for whom we'd care, and tie
bright ribbons in their hair.
All those dreams came true, for Tarn and Gwen.
But this is now and that was then
my daughter shrieks, picks up her pen –
words to blame and words to wound,
mightier, by far, than a sword.

I call to you, Ellan Vannin, my friend, who lived
so long ago. Long ago in a world of men: where
a magistrate picked up his pen. Wielding
his sword against your life, when you fell for
Greba, the magistrate's wife.

Till tomorrow then, and today I shall
bake fresh rolls, maybe take a walk, to the fields
on the hill, where the Phynodderree lives, the fairy
shepherd man, who rounds up wandering sheep
returns them home, reminds the farmers to
shut the gates.   I'll take lunch with me,
watch the ewes grazing,   listen to the silence,
live for today across   the healing bridge,
distanced from reality –
letters from a daughter in despair.

VI.

You stride the slopes of Slieuwhallion:
wind-shimmered grass sheens green
seawaves around the curve of the hill.
You and Greba, laughing light-heartedly,

your shawls pulled around you –
baskets over one arm for early gorse
for dyeing the wool. I hear the swish of
your garments, long kyrtils, gathered
at the waist by a belt, hear brittle twigs
snapping beneath the soles of your carranes.
Shivers run down my back.

I have been travelling onwards, forwards,
backwards, circling through time, towards you,
back to the fireside stories, faerie folk,
little fellows, giants and bugganes,
when some will say that here in our island,
our forebears trusted a pre-Christian trinity:
Leirr the unknowable source, sustainer of all being,
the ultimate abyss; *Aengus* the ever-young,
creative designer of love and life in action;
Mannanan, the wizard-king, mediator between
humanity and the unknowable.

Search the timelines, transpose from
our folklore, for we had our goddesses too:
Teeval, untouchable maiden-of-the-sea;
Morann, mother of Curoi, avatar
of Mannanan. Was she our most ancient
earth mother?

When strangers approach our island,
Mannanan throws his cloak of invisibility
around us all and a mist descends,
wrapping us, occluding us,
to protect us from our foes.
Through this mist I search for you,
on cloudy nights, when the moon is veiled.
I have to trust you: I know you are there.
You are holding me while I heal myself.
I am not to blame for

the cot-death of my grandchild.
I grieve for her, for you, Ellan Vannin,
for Greba Kelly, for all of us lost in a time-warp
in this folk-lore rich, mythical, sacred land.

Yours. Mine. This sacred isle, Mona's Isle,
through the eons she has been holy:
the Voyage of Bran recounts these truths
of the sacred isle, Ellan Sheeant, Inis
Seanta. We called our island the
Happy Place of Apple Trees, which is in Gaelic,
Eamhain Abhlach, and in Latin, Eubonia.

Yours. Mine. A place of pilgrimage, a
place of healing, a land of tranquillity
which was not always tranquil.
Our island was never afforded
the luxury of isolation :
tossed around in a stormy sea between the
Kings of Norway, Scotland, England.

I see ships approaching. Vikings with oars.
I see Mannanan fighting the invaders, himself a
three-legged wheel of fire, hurtling down
from his castle, the summit of Barrule.

I hear the beat of Viking oars, dip splash, dip splash,
like a drum beat, like a drum beat,
slicing open our ocean, ripping open our island,
cleaving open our women, plunder and pillage.

******

Cloudy morning in the silence of the Manx Museum,
I stand in awe among runes and dragons,
stone-carved, long lasting, swirls and curls,
triquetra knots, intricate, inter-laced,
communing coded messages from my ancient isle.

Then, I look up, as you arrive gently,
whispering with your fingertips,
rhythmic raindrops, tapping out time lines,
fingernails pattering the high glass roof.
You, Ellan Vannin, reaching me through glass,
as I hear myself respond:
ancestors ancestors bide with me bide with me
ancestors ancestors bide with me bide with me.

The archaeologists find our round houses
carbon date our organic remains
they themselves   remain
bewildered   uncertain   concerning
the chieftains' dwellings: a round puzzle.
Mannanan's cloak hides your full story,
your pre-patriarchal patterns - who could
comprehend this circularity - this roundness -
this roundness of our mothers,
this roundness of our goddesses,
this roundness of our wheel of time,
in the circles and the lives of our women,
in the homesteads of our foremothers,
when we were Ellan Sheeant's daughters?
ancestors ancestors bide with me bide with me
ancestors ancestors bide with me bide with me
Shall we lose count, Ellan Vannin,
numbering the turns of the spiral back around
these twists of fate ?
When were we the country ones - the goddess ones
celebrating our earth mother, our sea mother,
our sky mother, our moon mother:
how was it that we danced for them
and sang for them,
scribed our stories and buried our dead
and said : be glad each day we are
alive and wise - was it not that the first drums
were the women's drums?

ancestors ancestors bide with me bide with me
ancestors ancestors bide with me bide with me

Come home with me Ellan Vannin
I am going home to heal
Come woman time and settle in my bones again
Come to me home healing here
home in a small wooden house
on the edge of a green sea valley
in a green sea moor-land.
For were not the first drums the women's drums?
Heal the other parts of me
the other - the parts of m-other I might
have become if I hadn't become
Vorrie's mother's mother.

I rock myself in the arms of this moor-land
to the heart-beat heart-beat drum.
I understand this now while I am healing;
I understand this now while I am keening
for my grandchild and for your child,
Ellan Vannin.

Breathe steady steady steady
ready
ready to heal
beat a drum for me, Ellan Vannin.

VII.

In this small garden by the tree where
you buried your child, I pay respect to you,
as from the east, I notice that
a storm is gathering.

The night sky has fast moving cloud
the wind cuts through my clothes.

Enough light – until the distant rain arrives –
to know that   the hills are women
rounded   sleeping   waiting.
Here in this garden   while the storm moves
towards us   we witness you
me and the tramman tree
we know   we acknowledge.

You and Greba, holding one another,
looking into one another's eyes.
She loved the moon and she loved you
Ellan Vannin   she was in love
with you and you with her   you were real
you were beautiful   the two of you
she had always wanted children   adored
your baby daughter   she was her soul mother
she held you close when the baby died   you
were open, needy and vulnerable   she stayed with you
you wept on her breasts   you curled small   naked
in her arms   you were her child for a night or two
she was your mother   she was your child
you held one another   she was your lover.

Unfortunate for you, Ellan Vannin, to fall for
your woman friend. But who is to dictate to us
when and with whom, we may fall in love?
I imagine the magistrate, his skin-burning
discovery, his soul-searing resentment,
that her eyes were the same as yours –
and only shone for you.

I shudder to know him now. How he held his shame
inside. How it festered there like a sore
that wouldn't heal. How the poisons in his anger
burned like fever in his blood. How he slowly,
insidiously, planned his revenge.
He would sit at his desk in the long stone house

not wooden like yours – he was a man of substance –
a low long house with a thick turf roof – wielding his quill
against the independence of women like you,
the healers and the seers, with the Scandinavian gods
of revenge beckoning.
Of course the Viking invasions had long since ceased
and the Manx-Norse Kings lived in relative peace.
Their homesteads were Christian, at least in part,
but their vengeful warriors lived in their hearts.
The priests and the elders all were men and the
Diocese of Trondheim sanctioned them.

You were stricken with grief   your child was
dead - you began to dread
those men   who believed the words
from the magistrate's pen.

Then Greba Kelly begged
for your life. She was a good woman,
the magistrate's wife.
She flouted him to help you.
No, Ellan did not suffocate her baby.
She grieves for her child. She is desolate-
has not she been punished enough?
Her sing-song voice was raised in your defence.

At midnight under the waxing moon
I re-call the rules of those men of Rome.
You were despised by a man who spoke his lies.
He wanted you punished by the gods
of the skies.

On Ellan Vannin's life, the magistrate said - woman
whose child is suspiciously dead – the price is simple,
the body of my wife, nightly, forever, for the rest of
my life. Don't wince. If you want to save her life,
you come to me warmly as my wife.

Greba you're mine, my wedded wife, I hear you pleading
for your friend's life. Consider this. I'll save her life
but there'll be a price ...
You must be warm and welcoming in my bed.
You do not love me – this I know –
No matter so.
You will act like a wife and willingly be
warmly affectionate now to me. It is my decision.
It is my right.
You are my wife. I am your sire. You *will* obey me
in my bed - this is the price of your strange friend's head.
I will save the one whose child is dead
when you return to our marital bed.

I, Tarnagh, daughter of Morann, child of the storm,
can hear the magistrate writing his words,
muttering his script.
I can see him there, wielding the only power
he had left, over his wife.

I imagine you both, you and Greba, when the moon was full
at the stones – the circle at Maughold – it was
fatal to fall in love with your friend – such
a flaunting comfort when your child lay cold.
Your story's a tale of love and trust
beyond the magistrate's betrayal.
Yours is the healing power, the power of love,
you holding your beloved friend,
believing one another to inevitable end.

How you refused each of you to lie or be saved.
How she would not deny you   would not bed
with the man she no longer loved.
How the priests and elders reviled you.
How they honoured the words from the magistrate's pen.
How they went to the barrel maker.
How they ordered two oak barrels tall and stout.

How his hammer sounded, how the wood sounded.
How they went to the forge.
How the interior spikes sounded.
How the metal sounded.
How the iron-rimmed barrel sounded.
How they took you both then to the witches' hill.
How they blocked their ears from the sounds you made.
How they rolled you once
and rolled you twice and sent you
down the slopes of Slieuwhallion.

VIII.

Ellan Vannin, I have something to re-tell to you.
How they narrate, in the folk tales nowadays,
the story of Old Meg.
How she had foretold the fishermen of a storm
who took little heed – and met their harm – in our
boiling cauldron seas.
They blamed her for that self-same storm, said
Old Meg conjured the wind and rain.
They searched – they found a woman to blame.
Old Meg they placed in a barrel with spikes and
blocked their ears to the sounds inside.
Then they rolled her once and rolled her twice
and sent her down the slopes of Slieuwhallion.

IX.

Listen to the ocean, the ocean, the ocean,
listen to the women of your line reaching through:
back into the moor-lands, the hill farms, the
cliff walks, there on little island, your foremothers knew.

Tarnagh Callister, they call your name, they call your name:
they have on little island a story to unfold –
skim along the cloud ridge, fly to little island,

listen to your forebears: their song is very old.

Listen to the ocean, the ocean, the ocean –
they sing to you your heritage, a ballad from the soul –
you need not dread those hidden times, their voices, their call.
Sing their song of love and trust, then learn to name them all.
Do not fear to know them, their love is with you still,
there is healing on the island beside the witches' hill.
Of the line of Callister, born on little island,
the line of Callister – your foremothers knew –
farming folk and moor-land folk, their strength is with you still.

Listen to the ocean, the ocean, the ocean,
listen to the women of your line reaching down:
back into the moor-lands, the hill farms, the cliff walks,
the women of the island, their ways becoming known.

Listen to the ocean, the ocean, the ocean –
reach beyond the wound, the rage, to trust
the earth, the heart, the self,
to cease the storm, assuage the soul, to make you
voiced and whole again.

Calm tide and sea birds calling, calling, calling,
listen to the voices - your heart longs for peace.
Longing and belonging beside the witches hill.
Listen to the wise ones, whose strength is with you still.

Heal with Ellan Vannin in her valleys, on her moors,
beside her glens and rivers, her hills, her seas and shores.
Where she was where shall remain, alive, aware and strong.
Listen to the ocean, her early morning song.

1994 - 2007

Section Four

Northern Sojourn

The following series of poems tells the story of my leaving Cornwall in 1998 during the final breakdown of a disastrous relationship which had begun in 1992. One year later I met a lovely woman whom I have called here Clair de Lune.
Love is about recognising oneself in the mirror of beautiful others. It is about ordinary people capable of doing extraordinary things, day after day. I am deeply grateful to Clair de Lune. May she always find the love and healing she needs, for her love, though brief, gave me many gifts.

In particular it removed from my psyche the terrible images of war and power, which had haunted me by day and night, after the experience, in Cornwall, of having to flee from someone whom I had learned not to trust. The love from Clair de Lune removed those images, dissolved the night terrors, and gave me the confidence to dare to love Cynth Morris, now my life partner, when we reconnected as friends in the November that followed my midsummer adventure.

Flight
Shock Waves
Night Journey to Holywell Bay
Memory
The First Foal
When is the Right Time?
Truth
Moon Woman

Flight

Friendly voice: Come up here, girl,
we'll take care of you.
Thirteen and half hours on
long distance bus. One and a half hours
in a housing association office.
She again: Don't cry, girl. They're giving you
a flat, right.
They believe me. They believe me.

Enter my Bradford flat, close the door,
lean against it looking around. Sigh
with absolute relief.
No more bullying. No one monitoring my
phone calls. No cheating and lying
behind my back.
Four hundred miles
from that anguish. I am safe now.
Chosen to free myself.
Here is world class curry, music, culture,
landscape and cityscape.
Dozens of new lesbians
so maybe some new friends?
Here I can be.
Only fifty two.
Time to start again.

October 1998

Shock Waves

These feelings are real.
In the night, waking
reaching out to   nothing
no one.
So I will stand here
on the reality bridge,
calm myself,
tend my tub garden   alone
listen to the city sounds,
watch the cycles of the moon
changing herself.

I will observe urban trees withstanding
smoky summers, windy autumns,
city fumes, vehicle noise,
trundling traffic, lunging lorries.
These enormous trees, broad-leafed,
are changing themselves
holding me safely.

If they can, I can
change from within,
acknowledging my anniversaries,
staying true to myself,
welcoming my transformations,
getting on with my northern days,
talking with friends,
writing, writing, writing,
pages of words from
urban waysides, city night-times.

It is the only way I know to
live this new location,
calmly, quietly, hopefully,
wording it forwards.

Night Journey to Holywell Bay

Hundreds of miles from here
on some distant shore
in the dark of the moon
a sandy-floored cave
shimmers with a ring of candles.
Dancing hands shadow the walls
where rock-water runs from a
natural stone bowl
in a high-thighed crevice
while on the white black
waterline, low slow
waves murmur and retreat.

This night in a northern city
it is eerily quiet.
No sound of traffic.
No footsteps.
No voices.
Only the felt-footed tabby cats
and wide-winged owls
witness a west wind sweeping
clean this urban valley
invoking tidal memories
of its sea-sound familiars.

November 1998

Memory

Late night just falling asleep
warm, snug, relaxed.
Radio Four's worded comfort
gently cornering this inland attic
and anyway I like this room,
high eaves, sloping ceiling, roof lights,
soft terracotta carpet, a haven.

A wave of sound : ocean : I snap
awake and listen, trembling.
New series, four radio plays:
Earth Air Water Fire.

Tonight, story from Mousehole,
winter's wild seas, fishing fleets grounded,
boiling breakers beyond harbour's mouth,
a Cornish community starving, until
one skipper puts to sea, facing
force nine's full fury.

A hero returning, his nets heavy,
he feeds everyone, his bravery
never to be forgotten,
celebrated nowadays on
Tom Babcock's Eve, when
women bake fishes in Stargazey Pie.

My defenses breached, unable to resist
the ocean's power, I listen wet-faced
as peaks of memory, troughs of longing,
flow northwards, engulfing my bed.

Winter 1998-9

The First Foal*

Traditional Native Americans say:
the future is behind us.
In front of me, my recent past,
betrayal's pin-sharp details running
in a seamless, ceaseless, sound and motion
loop, on a great impenetrable screen.
Me traded-in for a younger model,
less disabled, more wealthy.
Take a kitchen knife, the sort to cut
fresh herbs, you know the sort of knife.
Cut a hole in that enormous screen,
step neatly through to summer woodlands
the other side.

One day in May, I take the herb knife,
part the patterns of swirling light. Cut
clear a route, step through, away,
my journey unframed, my movements
freer, unconstrained. A healing hologram
of future time made and re-made, by intention,
from moments of now.

***

I drive to the farm very excited - about
to meet a brand new earth creature.
The drive itself represents freedom, independence,
forgiveness: my car, a gift from my older son.

Unconditional love, from both my sons,
now in their late twenties, a
sustaining, empowering presence.

Driving by cotton grass and windswept sheep
my mantra begins: Nine and seven: they were
only nine and seven.
My mantra continues: nine and seven; nine and seven.
Mantra, a voice, a circle, a ring of time.
A new-born foal: this baby, my babies.
The mother bond intense this afternoon.

Warm and loving, both my sons,
circle of redemption, of acceptance:
Their love to give me courage – dare go on,
go forward, stay open to the Now.

The women appear,
from a barn, gloriously dirty,
building in the roof all day –
heavy duty filthy task.
Emerging laughing, hug me gingerly
lest muddy me up!
Strange, I feel shy, shy of the women,
shy of their bereavement this past year,
shy of meeting my first foal.

***

I am to hold a handful of your baby food.
Rattle tin buckets to bring your mother,
so you will arrive behind her. You go
where-ever she goes. You come
when-ever she comes.
Now, suddenly, you are here.

I am entranced, but, being human,
show too much emotion,
not quiet and steady.
You back away.
'Be calm. Very still. He is a wild animal.

He has to learn to trust you.'
Swiftly, I recall learned stillness waiting
for rabbits to play on Cornish cliffs; long
silences watching undisturbed buzzards
hover, rise, playing the thermals. First
moments with my kittens. Holly would
not bond – Solly trusted from first contact –
I fell in love – his function was
to purr – he loved people, absolutely.
Hologram swirls, grief smacks me across
the mouth – he lives in Cornwall – have
not held him for months. Betrayal spins
as pain engulfs.

Now you are here. I have to learn how
to be. You are an oblong by design,
a breast-high shoe-box on tall
spindle-legs. A Walt Disney
creature, though strong-boned,
solid, stouter than Bambi, you're
a perfect neatly-formed baby horse.

For your sake I ground my energy,
slow my breathing, stand so quietly.
You allow me to touch you.
You are exquisitely beautiful, but I
beware your Mom's huge hooves.
Could break my foot
with one false step.

They teach me to kneel beside you,
one hand firmly around your bum,
the other reaching over, holding
behind your head.
I begin to know you. Your strong firm body
pulsates, warmly, against me,
my face leans into you,

the palm of my right hand
contacts your rough hairy rump.

Your body is so close: I am wrapped around you,
you are my music, my guitar. You allow
our two beings to blend - the
life force in you reaches to me -
your body heat radiates through me.

The mother in me flips to London:
my first baby, four a.m.: my hand cradles
Mark's head – his eyes unfocussed, his fontanel
so vulnerable: a sensuous bonding.
The mother in me flips again - to a dim
dining room, suburban terrace,
falling in love with my second baby,
three in the morning, he and I,
Madonna and child, firelight, Debussy's
Clair de Lune.

My hand is pressed against the hair
of a new foal's buttock: The lover in me
fast-tracks to urban settings: a purple
bedroom in a Brixton squat:
a hotel bedroom in Brighton: a weaver's
warehouse on the Thames; the curve
of my hand rounds a woman lover's mound,
the skin of my palm recalls warm pubic hair –
in one moment all through me –
a womb-lurch-longing for that
intimacy sometime, somewhere, again.

My left arm enfolds your head, delicately
sculptured with a white blaze down your nose.
I see wild horses running in old Europe,
their manes flying in the wind,
dust rising from their hooves, as they curve,

swerve, past the yellow gorse at the mouth
of a foaming river.

New born foal, are you Epona's child?
Great horse goddess, avatar of the Amazons'
horse mother, who birthed you in the spirit
of all wild creatures, with a longing to be free.
Epona, she of the rushing waters: listening,
I hear a nearby stream, a child-river gurgling,
laughing, tumble-jumbling its route down hill
to meet its mother.
But in your form and beauty I begin to know
all your mothers, for there are many.

A woman has died, mourned throughout
this region, your spirit mother, creating you
first in her human imagination. She wanted you.
You were her idea. She dreamed you,
designed you, chose your parents.
Her spirit imbues this place. She breathes
here in every blade of grass;
in every leaf on the woodland trees.
Through each petal on each flower
each vegetable in the tended plots,
she brings love and healing to the women.
The warmth of her spirit is in every hair
on your body. You are named from her.
Carry forward her living energy.
Even I, almost a stranger, can feel it.

Sacred mare, Epona, bestowed sovereignty
in Celtic rituals of kingship: in rites of
marriage with the mare-goddess.

Epona's child: are you now a fertility gift
for this community? Shall all the women
become your mothers: each woman a

different aspect of your sentience: your joy of
dancing – no-one can dance quite
like a tiny foal; your laughter – I didn't know
horses would leap for joy; your healing
contact – me with my arms around you;
your involvement in this landscape.
Are your dark brown eyes reflections
of the eyes of Clair de Lune? Hers have
deep peat pools of a mature woman's
wild grief; yours are merely filled with
liquid babyhood.

You have not known grief, not yet, but are
there questions, wild-creature in your heart:
'Can I trust these women? Who are all
these mothers here?'
As for me, kneeling in this hologram
with you, I span bridges over teaming
waters tumbling with my Celtic questions.

Your conception, arranged by humans?
I think not. Field gates were opened.
Your parents met - no interest.
Mare and stallion passed by, snubbed
the human plans. Feigned indifference.
Waiting, maybe, for a private moment?
Visible portents, neighbourhood anecdote,
a well-told tale: how a double rainbow,
crystalline and perfect, appeared to herald your
conception. How the women laughed, gave
your second name, Rainbow, the
ultimate gay cliché.

I knew I had to see you. The miracle
of you, your perfect newness. You will grow
quickly - these moments are rare. Time to be
very still, watch and learn.

Like you, I arrive, near new women,
allow them a glimpse of myself.
Droplets of time that hold together
in one moment all the possibilities
of past, present and future.

I hold you in my arms, new-born foal,
two weeks old, how broken dreams heal
and life begins again. How my loss
be transformed from a solid barrier of pain
into a swirl of light and colours
that somewhere, sometime,
I can step though, to a healing place,
even if only for a moment,
where my dreaming bridge touches
solid ground, here in the Now.

Quiet for a moment, holding you, my first foal,
looking across a deep-sided valley,
grieving for my lost women's land,
my millennium woodlands, my baby trees,
my Cornish headlands, my raging seas,
I have an incredible sense of 'land' –
the spirits of place.
Earth energy up through my feet,
open air, wind in old trees,
sunlight and wide skies,
a newly planted memorial woodland,
a stream rushing down to a river.

I was the mother of a woodland:
A thousand trees, my grand design.
Am I destined always to give birth
then leave? Children and trees.
Consult the ancestors, multiple strands.
Norse-folk dreaming spectrum
words or pictures from sky mother's

necklace, name this a rainbow bridge
one and the same, messengers
transporting sky wishes to the earth.

Me, here, holding you, my first foal.
Across time and space, European myths
and legends collide, elide, in holographic
splendour: escape from Mora, night terror,
death horse, a living nightmare.
Invoke Rhiannon: blamed for her actions,
carrying burdens on her back, mother
with a male child, until, absolved,
she re-invents herself, horse woman,
faster than the speed of light,
source of all Elysian joy
she turns her life round
to start over.

1999-2006

*This narrative poem was first read to the women on the farm that
healing summer of 1999. I then filed it, for several years, only returning
to it for this collection. Meantime my elder daughter-in-law, Katherine,
told me I'd enjoy Philip Pullman's trilogy, His Dark Materials. I did so
without remembering this poem. Then I discovered, March 2006, in
the original draft of The First Foal, my experience of cutting a hole in
the world, stepping through. I should not be surprised, as a Celt, that so
many other human beings employ, and enjoy, this imaginative device.

When is the Right Time?

I – had given myself
at least
one more year
before
allowing such a thing
to happen.

You – are only a few months
from devastating loss.

But is the loneliness supposed to go on
and on in linear time?
Is there ever a right time, to ask
for a spiral curl?

Is it possible just
to accept this wonderful meeting,
to allow it and our healing power,
enclosing and encompassing
all of your history and all of mine –
the past, the present,
and each other?

Summer 1999

Truth

I am going to dare　　　truth dare truth dare
to tell you:
The truth, the whole truth, and nothing but the truth.
It began as Compassion, and slid
irretrievably into Love.

That's the truth of it. It won't move over
conveniently into Friendship.
If it would, I could relax and rest,
my mind peaceful, my dreams undisturbed.
I've tried all that – No can do:
Not this time, this loving.

I'll be creative with it, stay friendly,
attempt to do nothing unwise.
I won't act inappropriately – I will be strong,
getting on with my life, not waiting on yours.

By all means wait for Clair, says my counsellor,
wait for next summer, or the summer after that,
if needs be.
But don't wait for joy in your life,
plant flowers now that are in flower now,
dance, be glad, wake each day
and tell the world you are okay.
Because you are.

Love doesn't come easy – the price is high.
It doesn't fade easy – this one won't.
That's the truth of it.

September 1999

Moon-woman

I write this for the woman whose touch
made me feel beautiful again;
I write to make sense of it all.
I write to heal; to comprehend her
presence; to try to understand;
to attempt to live through
all the chances, all the changes.

How it feels to love someone
who cannot respond. How we were
until panic set in and she flew away.
How she fled from me – went to live
the other side of the moon.

Now she has become the woman
in the moon. I watch her cycles
of wax and wane, ebb and flow.
Beautiful, unattainable, inaccessible.
I read her moods occasionally as she
comes and goes.

Sometimes, in her dark phase,
I begin to comprehend.
Other times, I am aware of her
growing full and splendid, until
the passing of the clouds suddenly
masks her face.
Obscured or full-bodied, she continues
her journey, her cycle of transformation.

On sleepless nights, I lie awake in the dark,
my room lit by moonlight. Then I watch
her movement, across the night skies.
I whisper her name to myself, hold my
lonely arms around my solitary body,

lying here without her.
She has to take the time and space
she needs, orbiting the night so far
away from me.

Grief is not, in any case, a linear process.
Her cycles of bewilderment, anger,
depression, despair, acceptance,
do not fit neatly with calendrical time.
My moon-woman, my gone-from-me lover
dwells in elipses, framed in dark
branches of midnight trees.

I must not call to her, nor shout her name.
I shall be strong. I will contain
my grief behind this glass.
My mourning the loss of her
must not disturb her. She does not need
my grief, my offensive intrusion
on her own bereavement.
But my loss is real just the same.
It is mine: I feel it, know it, cuddle
its chill in the lonely hours before dawn.

She was my midsummer lover, warm and strong.
She was my land-woman,
my earth-woman, my dancing partner,
her body alive and passionate beside me.

Now she resides on a silver-white
sky-floating stone. She has become
my moon-woman-sky-dweller,
whose distant reflected light
so coldly chills me, pulling my body tides,
tugging my feelings. I lie on my empty bed,
allowing her moonlight to fall on
my bare skin, my night lover in the sky.

Gone.

She flies a lonely sojourn,
nightly searching the heavens
for the signs and sounds
of the woman she still loves.

I am not the one for whom she grieves.
Moon-woman's sorrow could fill the oceans.
Such is the depth of it, the length of it,
the necessary time of it.
My summer-lover has flown up, up and away
from me, up into the night mirrors; skimming
her sky pathways; diving down through
deep oceans, spiralling again re-cycling
up, up and away, away from me, sky-floating
the winds of time.
Leaves me hurting, nowadays,
with only this moonlight playing itself
over my un-passioned skin.

Sometimes moon-woman slips through the veil,
to lure me onto dangerous shores.
Sometimes her echo assumes
a low seductive tone, redolent with
our erstwhile intimacy, its timbre suggestive,
potential re-construction.
Perhaps moon-woman, who once was
my earth-woman, carries a fragment
of embers, small glimmer of earth-core,
that still wants and needs me,
an un-faded spark.

Foolishly, still in love, I enter
the tidal pull moon spell. Wade into
waves that rattle on the sand.
Forgetful of weeds and broken bottles,

I blend with the water that is pulled
by the moon, until splattered with sharp
glass edges against my bare flesh,
my wounds are re-opened.
Blood drains into sand, colouring
the waves by moonlight.
Held momentarily, in moon-woman's gaze,
I am in dangerous ebb-tides, washing out to sea.
Rip tides, undercurrents, no security
at the ocean's edge, only the flotsam
and jetsam on the sucking sand,
fragments of old photos that speak
happier times, the feel of her, the sound
of our laughter during
her holiday from grief.

Who will she hold, when she returns?
Who will I be by then? How will be
my own journeys? Will I still be standing
here, this very same place
at the edge of the tide? I should not.

Who will have walked beside me? Who will have
held me, comforted me, warmed me?
I cannot know.
Odyssey. I search for how to move on.
Inside me lies my own healing power.
No one else can do this for me.
I have to do this by myself.
I have to do this for myself.

Inside I am as beautiful as moon-woman
because I know how to love,
through all time and changes.
I can grow and transform
like moon-woman: I do not have to deny
my heart, even though she cannot respond.

Now I must search the triple aspect:
Crone woman, who guides me forward;
Mother woman, who gives and receives love;
Young woman, the hopeful one,
the girl who can play.

Three for one and one in three:
I must be for me.
Alive, aware and strong, I will try to love again.
Lonely it's true, but shining, this healing
held, inside me.

October 1999

Section Five

The Chakra Sequence

It was during a drumming workshop with Ova music group in the nineteen eighties that I first came across the concept of the energy centres of the body, which are known as "chakras" in Eastern medicine. In the music workshop I was taught that the chakras respond to different energy wavelengths, or frequencies, which can be represented in both sound (music) and colour. I decided to learn more about colour healing and healing with music and natural sounds such as the wind and the ocean. So important did this become to me in terms of how my body stays well, fit and energised that throughout my career in women's studies and women's creative writing, I taught my students about these energy centres. In my women's studies and creative writing classes, we used movement, meditation and music, alongside extracts of women's writings, to free our energies and enable creative discussion and expression.

When I was very ill in the late nineteen eighties, with Chronic Fatigue Syndrome, my body responded negatively to many kinds of energy vibrations, including electrical and magnetic vibrations and all kinds of traffic vibration. This meant that I was dying in Greater London's conurbation and that the move to Cornwall, with my then partner Keri Woods, was life saving. But later, after Keri and I had separated in 1992, I had entered a disastrous lesbian relationship, from which I fled from Cornwall to Bradford, in 1998, taking a gamble that my body could cope again with being in an urban environment. Emotionally Bradford was wonderful for me, giving me music, wonderful food, access to the Yorkshire Dales, and loving sustaining new friendships. Chakra healing is about balance, and that includes the right balance of relationships, not just the immersion in the natural world, or an over-simplified concept of wilderness.

My older son currently studies Tai Chi, in which the whole system of exercise is based on the energy centres being cleared. These days my understanding of chakra energies is a source of joy and freedom to me, both creatively and sexually. Towards the end of 1999, whilst living in Bradford, I re-met Cynth Morris, whom I had first known ten years previously. Subsequently I wrote this sequence for her.

Treasures – the Red and Orange Chakras
Light a Yellow Candle – the Solar Plexus
The Heart Chakra is Green
Healing in Blue – the Throat Chakra
Visions – the Magenta Chakra
Lavender – the Crown Chakra

Treasures

Between my hip bones safe, smiling, warm,
lives a pulsating   bowl of ruby light
whose sides are   woven with orange
and red, moving,   so slowly spinning
magma energies   of earth with fire
smiling my days   towards passionate
nights, whence   forth come images,
words, songs and   mysteries. In this
bowl I re-create   the letters of your
name, carving its   consonants from
gleaming black   Welsh coal. In
this bowl I keep, in old Welsh gold,
your mother's signet ring.

In this centre   we conjoin our
Celtic times   where my past
possibilities   touch you, my
woman-lover   friend 'n future,
blending with   you, my beloved,
  in our sensuous   moments of now;
    here now I hold you, your essence
         scenting me fragrant
              in old musk.

Light a Yellow Candle

There was a time – not so long ago –
when I was grieving,
lost, lonely.

Inside my solar plexus –
a cold, sad centre
my middle chakra – weeping a little,
a long northern winter ahead.

Now, since you, my darling,
the healing is tangible.

In that same yellow zone
there is your warmth,
the sound of your laughter,
us driving on
sunlit roads,
long shafts of light
playing across
winter's early resting fields.

Hotel table, tiny glass lamp,
a wick into
yellow oil, very thin,
translucent as sunlit water.
Glass nozzle,
miniature
yellow
flame,
bright, alive, steady.
You speak of
summer gardens, scented roses,
yellow daisies, gladioli,
double begonias, delicate posies.
Golden reflections, lazy

waters, warm sand,
Australia.
Sunshine.

Meanwhile we wait –
north and south.
Shall use my days
for writing,
fill my nights
with friends.
Shall light a yellow candle
by the telephone.
Golden flames –
trustworthy words.
Your loving voice
to hug me warm.

The Heart Chakra is Green

Part One: Myself

Last autumn, in this northern city
I lived without a garden. No earth to dig, no
plot to love, no plants to tend, and no one
to hug me. There was a hole behind my ribs,
the re-opening of a heart wound, the anger
of a woman betrayed.

Last autumn, with shiatsu, I began the healing.
I swam, letting the water hug me; I line danced,
allowing the music to hug me – and you don't need
a partner for that; I walked in the city, so that
the light from festive windows would hug me;
I walked in the hills, where the
slanting December sunlight could hug me.

I watched the mighty oaks shedding toxins
returning them to the earth. The spirits of the
trees spoke silently: we can withstand the city,
the pollution, the noise, the rubbish, the lack
of care. If we can do it, so can you. Put down
your roots. Learn from us – use this time –
you will experience joyful growth
in the greening of the spring.

I was solitary, the wounded healer. Alone:
trying to be strong. I was not always strong.
Not everyday, strong.
I bought some tiny red metallic hearts and stars –
one for my fridge door each day survived in an
urban landscape. If I did two hundred it would
carry me to the spring.

I did it. I did it a day at a time. I did it an hour
at a time. I could do it again, if I had to.
The hole in my back is mended.

Part Two: Yourself

I want you to be held safely, by me,
held the way that a friend is held,
relaxed and warm, knowing that you are free
to find out who you are and what you want to be.
I want you to experience the green of living –
no more broken hearts, like the Labi Siffre song.
I want you to wake each morning feeling
lightweight, loved and loving,
contented but stimulated and encouraged
in the things you'd like to learn.
When you look inside your body, in your lungs
and around your heart I want you to see
clear green light, as if you could breathe
inside an enormous green leaf on a tree
in warm summer sunlight.
I want every blade of green grass under your
bare feet in summer to be smoothed soft
for you to walk on, an easy companionable life
with me, as if someone painted a smile across
your shoulders and held your heart gently,
very gently in green hands – like the tenderest
plant that should be treated with special care.
I want you to know that you are held in
esteem, honoured and respected by me
for the work that you do, the sports that
you enjoy, and the woman that you are.
Whatever you are being or doing
I want you to find that life opens up
gladly for you, and when you sleep

that your dreams are of beautiful gardens,
with delightful streams and everything
balanced, enough of all that you need, and…
so much love that you never feel lost,
lonely or afraid, not ever again, my darling.

Healing in Blue – the Throat Chakra

Open-throated now that I am with you,
I discover that I can voice anything,
or everything, murmur sweet nothings, reveal
my blue secrets without threat. My words are
free flowing now, because this loving is our
magical mystery tour through
communication routes to Celtic wisdom.
Speaking all the time, phone lines, emails: we both love
to share, to show and tell, to learn what is
the best we can each become.

In my mind I dance where the wide blue waters
meet the shore, dreaming the Mabinogion,
entranced by you and your Celtic passions:
you desire to walk by moving water.
Blue upon blue, the line penned thick on the
distant horizon holds my vision of infinity -
loving you for ever - while we are held
temporarily, in the earth's circle.

When we are old I want to sail
with you in a blue boat
powered by the wild blue wind across
the waves to Tir na Nog or
The Blessed Isles.

Meanwhile in this life time we could fly over
blue mountains, holiday by blue lagoons.
We are free as blue birds to do what we need to
become wise and happy and strong.
And I will fill your days with blue flowers and
your nights with blue moons. I will whisper words
of deep blue loving, and pleasure you in
soft blue sheets with scented pillows.
A blue boat carries my song onwards.

Visions – the Magenta Chakra

Sitting semi-naked at my computer
wearing only
my magenta velvet coat
like Colette in the bath
wearing only
her hat.

My coat is tactile – crushed padded
velvet, with satin buttons – swirled
shades of purple, magenta, deep plum,
black-currant, indigo and deep red wine.
Colours of the third eye – the visionary
energy centre in the middle of our
foreheads – from whence we know things,
the womb-eye synthesis.

Did you know that cunnit was
the verb 'to know';
cunt was the source of all wisdom;
a cunning woman was
'she who was infinitely wise'?

You speak to me of rainforests
my own deep caverns moist and warm.
You touch me there and colours fly my mind
like exotic birds of paradise
feathered flight upon feathered flight
in the high canopies
dappled by tropical sunlight.

We work to save ourselves from destruction
to give and receive love and healing
with hands on affection;
to save our families from hurt and pain
to give them comfort and nurturing

support through life's exigencies.
We work to save the lesbian community
and damaged women everywhere – new
ways of being for each other in groups:
our vision is culture, community and continuity.
We work to save the planet from destruction
challenging de-forestation, demanding the end
to pollution in gardens, waysides,
farms and parks. We plant new woodlands
and organic orchards:
we work, we work, we work.

When the working day is done and
winter evenings close around us
we reach with vision and open hearts,
warm mouths and loving hands to one another,
you and I re-designing a world that
we feared we had lost and have found again.

I sit here semi-naked, in my tactile velvet coat
like Colette in the bath
wearing only her hat.
With you in my life, my darling, there is
nothing I cannot en-vision.

Lavender

The power of the crown chakra
harnessed by my Manx ancestors:
shaman-women spiralling through other worlds
unboundaried. Time-limitless transport –
go-anywhere-be-anything essence of self.

Healing herb fringing the paths of
Sissinghurst, Llangollen –
old dykes have walked those
beloved gardens, hand-in-hand,
passionate friends,
consciously calling upon
spirits of place.

Wild fragrant herb of my island,
hand-gathered, bunch-dried,
my grandmother's kitchen:
lavender scented linen,
folded, flattened, aired,
ironed, stored in iron-doored
closets, with slatted floors,
above her old black-leaded range.

I and my birth-land divested of our
cloaks of invisibility, infinity fathoms
our moonlit waters, where mythic
maidens merge with Celtic matriarchs:
then Faerie glens descend, redolent with mysteries,
by swift streams to splash to shingle beaches.
Songs of mermaids repel thunder of Bugganes
from Old Barrule: I read runes from the north,
and Icelandic messages from the first
millennium.

I hold you all – images, ancestors,
loved ones, dreams – inside my skull –
just below the crown –
call upon you when I need you
journey with you via this lavender pathway,
wherever, whenever, I must.

Return to this moment here now rejoice
that, for many decades, we lesbians have
named this colour as, indeed,
our own.

Section Six

Home at Last

In 2005, Cynth Morris and I found Owl Cottage, a very tiny urban dwelling with a very large garden in East Devon, only twenty minutes by car to Britain's famous Jurassic coast. Here we feel settled and very happy, making new friends and busy with our work and network of women friends in this beautiful region. I am taking myself by surprise – so enjoying living in an urban location – I who once longed to inhabit a rock in the Atlantic. My Chronic Fatigue is long gone, though it hovers now and then to remind me. We have one bedroom and one office indoors, and I work in a converted shed-shack in the garden.

Hello Boys
Mother-in-law
Crone Mirror
Coast
Buddleigh Salterton
Dancing with Demons
Focus on Love
A Room of One's Own
Awakening
I Believe in Miracles

Hello Boys

I don't have any answers –
Still full of questions
even though
I'm sixty now
Can't turn back the clock
but would I do it again?
How can I tell?
From here, from this place of healing
loving you, both my married sons
bringing me joy and life and hope:
more questions.

It hurt.   It hurt us all.
What I did.   What I had to do.
Do it, or die, was the feeling.
So I did it for a time, separatism, and always loved you
from inside me, deep, deep inside.
But politics means prices.
Security, yes, they do say that separatism was
the only continuity
the women's movement ever had,
but what could you do about the boys?

Image of a night-time cave
a stony hillside, wide warm valley
both my tiger cubs asleep on straw
me by the entrance, tending a fire.
Eyes darting, I wouldn't let them harm you
kept you always from any woman who might tell you
all men were bad, boy children were aliens.
Wouldn't let them near you, would have walked through
fire to protect you, from some other women.
Did walk through fire.
Glandular fever, fire in the blood.

Yes there was a contradiction.
My politics and you –
that's what tore me in two –
leaving you and loving you.

Now I have gained two very amazing young women
as the wives of my sons.
Me?   Yes, me, who said she didn't agree with marriage
that age-old institution supporting the
Patriarchy.
I had those many words to learn, you know.

I still don't have any answers
never ever could stop loving you
never tried didn't want to stop
just went on grieving
and trying to be me.

Sometimes I look at my woman
and in my mirror
        mirror on the wall
and back again   at my woman   and think
if only   if only and what if?
What if we'd met age seventeen and twenty two?
Had a child each, the both of you.
But then you wouldn't be you
would you?
You're my be-loveds, the sons of
a man I dearly loved
when I was very young
when heterosexuality was what there was
or loneliness.

So here we are
and I still love you.
More, every day,
and I'm glad.

November 2006

Mother-in-law

Am I really old enough to be a mother-in-law?
Am I wise enough to love, give, mind my own business?
I loved my own mother-in-law:
Warm, welcoming, keeping house in trad style –
she the heart, he the head, and 'they-both' devoted.
As you walked into her home
the cares of the world fell off your shoulders:
something to live up to.

Me and my woman can we be there, when these young women
need us?
Can we love and cherish, accept and encourage
two fabulous young women
partners of my sons?

One juggles work and love, politics and philosophy,
studying and saving the planet;
names herself a feminist – so, glory be –
we hear again the F word
reassuringly close to home.
Two goes mountain biking
when she's not snowboarding,
amazes me with her capability,
juggles work and home, love and family
wants to be lots of fun
and a child-centred mum.

Being real, I laugh at myself, still there,
with my folded up soap-box. Me here digging
this garden; where now my second phase
women's movement
with its glories and challenges,
prices, and forms of martyrdom?

Bathroom mirror, white-haired woman with a pink-red face
I don't mind how I look but they have no inner image
of me, brown-haired creamy-skinned.
To them I look like this.

If they are that age, early thirties, then I must be this age,
early sixties, which is quite amazing really:
the cliché question: where did it go?

How it goes now is loving both my sons,
chalk and cheese, and loving their wives,
who are warm, welcoming, getting on with it,
who, earthly gifts, see in my sons what I see,
but as lovers not as mothers.
My mother-in-law long gone, my turn now.
Lucky in love, that's me, so am I old enough
and wise enough, now?

2007

Crone Mirror

Who was that young woman full of angst, quoting statistics
on world inequality, burning with fire for women's liberation,
yearning with passion for woman-loving philosophies?
I hug her sometimes, remind myself
I am so grateful for the journey.
Other times I visualise my inner self:
taught myself to crone travel
all through this body, each and every cell, every chakra,
body-house-work, throwing out the rubbish, cleaning tidying
sorting recycling conserving weaving patching mending
learned it long ago   when inner healing was
do it or die: there it is   inside me,
a crone mirror,
see myself again   striped with words   through
each long bone   like seaside rock:
Lesbian.

Joyful word   recognition smiles
into the night dark   heart leaps lovely high
skips as if a girl-child is finding shiny wrappers,
hidden candies. All ages of woman child mother
girl mature-one integrated, blended, pick'n mix.

I ponder the past the present the future
ask serious questions: ask them for fun too
what if I'd never loved women, (what a waste,
you cannot be serious) hadn't left my husband,
or my little boys – hadn't had to put any of them
through that – hadn't wanted to hadn't had to hadn't chosen to,
but that woman couldn't become me,
could she?

February 2007

Coast

Small rescue Collie cross Russell
bounding turns happily ensures we're
still with her striding by green cornfield's margins
wide stony big sky coast path to Ladram
tall pines behind us collage a cliffline
Buddleigh's beach becomes shingle spit
thick rushed slow moving salt marsh
where reflective waters ripple through
reeded silted estuary nature reserve
bird hides and sanctuary
shimmering heat ahead of us
scarlet poppies scramble an old stile
white marguerites soften tumbled boundaries
we collect fallen feathers observe
vermillion stars scattered among wild heartsease
share sweet apples listen as a skylark rises
rapidly beyond mere human vision into hot sunshine
surprising early holiday makers enjoying this
Mediterranean April in Devon scanning cloudless
skies we can hear invisible skylark
but witness only a skein of wild geese winging

Small rescue Collie cross Russell skipping ahead
joyfully embodies our feelings
she isn't a large fantastic Alsatian
nor do we need four rabbits a barn or an oak tree
old yearnings long gone
here now delighted
new dreams made real

April 2007

Buddleigh Salterton

Women lovers have walked this beach
hand in hand rambling the Jurassic coast
rose-red sunsets   crumbling sandstone cliffs
billions of beach stones
riverbed deposits
rolled rotated tumbled into smooth flat pebbles   dragged over
vast deserts
inside a fast flowing river
traversing the Triassic.

So, walking, we are crunching numbers:
but here you left your truck, Annie, with its keys
for the police   here you ran onwards barefoot into ten foot
waves
those rocking and rolling seas it was a tough love
ocean those rough November days.

You knew the sea, were you swimming strongly onwards to
join the ocean mother   how far to the indigo deep did you go
did you know that the rip tides or coastal currents would carry
you home   did you plan to send us just that one brief
message:
A foot on Chesil beach
(that's a fair distance down this coast)
and where are your other bones now ?

Loved your sea-blue-green eyes, Annie
we loved you so short a time bouncing into our lives laughing
joking mile a minute crying your story in hot wet tears returning
home alone and lonely to your three am night-stallion shadows.
Just one foot on Chesil beach to tell us that
you meant it
said you'd do it and indeed you did
this time   oh this time   you did you did.

I cannot tell your story in this one
brief poem how it was for us loving you how it is
for all of us now
only a novelist could do that for you, Annie
and I will   indeed I will I will.

Winter 2006-2007

Dancing With Demons

Women's Press gone no take over bid
not part of worldwide
publishing house
nothing left but
silence.

Wake each night through two a.m. dark
watch wordless cast of glittering demons
choreographed in midnight rehearsals
slip with them into fancy footwork
we all of us in black leotards
red ears silver Doc Marten boots
long tails red with arrow tips.

Wild fabulous demons what if and if only
with faces but lipless, with tails but tale-less
with necks but no mouths, with throats but no voices.

This wordless no place
between
publishing contracts
vast limbo mind space, continuous silence
bewildering confusion
what if words never return?
what if no one ever listens ever again?

Dancing with demons night by night
till
Bush and Blair choose to plummet
western bombs
into Middle Eastern homes.

Head splitting anger
recall Oslo's peace museum –
Jimmy Carter's words ring

hollow sand dune echoes:
You cannot make peace by
killing other people's children.

Shaken from silence
do something!

March against Iraq war one of hundreds
one of thousands okay to be ordinary
with two million ordinary others
special people ordinary people
especially extraordinarily angry.
Grandmothers babies uncles sons
wheelchairs nieces aunties granddads
families friends   every color height
size shape creed   me my son my
daughter-in-law two lesbian friends
from Oslo.

Pictures arrive, pictures, yes, many, worldwide,
contour maps of Iraq, bombed-out Bagdad,
Basra, the northern towns.

Inside Iraq another woman cannot sleep
rises carefully creeps to kitchen
facing night   bomb bard   ment
bombs noisy
bards wordy
ment
meant to shatter maim frighten terrify subdue
bring oil revenue
multiple bombing multiplies semantics
demon-bombs are lexicons
sky-diving questions
will my family survive this night's
bombardment? where will we find clean
water? how will we dispose of sewage? who will

transport food from the fields? whose body lies
by this bombed-out truck? will you bury her? can
you place a placard, write the car number, so her
relatives may find her? is this your wife?
your sister? your niece? your daughter? does not
every civilian know someone who seeks someone?
men, women, children: shall we count five hundred
bodies a day in this bombardment here? can you
hear me in your western kitchen? this night that you
cannot sleep? are you dancing with your demons?
mine are different – our night terrors are carnage,
somebody screaming, children crying,
all of us afraid.
Oh how
luxurious would be your
wordless
devon-demoned-dark.

Late spring 2003

Focus on Love

Focus on love
It will carry me through
Through the times when
Armageddon seems nearer
Than in Cadfael's era
Focus on the play of light and shade
Tree shapes stretching across the garden
Focus on the bright green
The in-between
Don't lose heart even though
They keep on murdering
Plundering
Wanting what others have
Claiming revenge
Avenging
When everywhere is war, terror
Rain and fog
When they tell you the vast numbers
Of disasters impending
Populations affected
The climatic changes
The endangered species
The irreversible trends
Focus on love
When you don't know what to do
For the best
In politics
Ecology, wastefulness
Focus on love
Reach out, phone a friend
Hug someone, smile at anyone
For any reason
Keep on going
Don't give in, don't give up
Focus on love.   November 2006

A Room of One's Own

Wind from the west   blue bright skies
mill-race full swollen   we seek the otter who evades
us   slinking upstream invisible
back in my garden
hidden here   behind the high street   magical secret
so exciting   my own writing cabin
lined insulated recycled walls recycled windows   recycled shed
indeed   already a Montana wraps around my roof   same
old warm brown-gold wooden shed door   rough hewn planks
sloping ceiling   high shelves banked with poetry   folklore
history seed packets
whilst beyond dolphin window honeysuckle
creeps confused   in late abundance
of fluffed fragrance
cream-white   despite November

week one of our Celtic year
I scribe Friday afternoon sleepy
overlooking a playtime weekend garden   remains of
Sunday's full moon fire   old pear prunings with
garden gleanings   each day's awakening in early
pouring light   south-east dawning floods our bedroom
new every morning
alive well-woman and strong   no hint of fatigue
ready each day to wake up get going a day's writing
anticipating again
winter's dark creative deep   observe one golden rose
fourth flowering in one summer's growth   again
blossoms   she heralds global warming's
tepid winter days   though by night
black skies reach to iced infinity
with sequinned stars the full cliché   so magnolia gathers her
strength   for winter's challenge   her buds
now fur-muffed fingers   but plummeting thermometers
pearl-frost the bookstore roof

my liberation – a phone in a garden shack

It's Mark's voice – Katherine may travel   he may join her
she craves again Indonesia   their lives shared their love
profound   their process complex   meant to be   she
and he   travel onwards   full of questions   how should
we   how can we   in the twenty-first century   be?

It's Rob's voice – just married   plays five-a-side football studies
his masters   Sophie plans snowboarding   mountain
biking anything extreme   they are happy   he is happy
my soul flies high   images of his wedding   London cabbies
the flowers   the marquee big red bus   the fun of it all
all of us onwards   to the evening singing 'wheels on the
bus go round and round' laughing   ready to dance
full-on wedding-fun   for my
younger son   happiness is…

Winter 2006-7

Awakening

Awakening in a safe
light bedroom   my ears
record   the breathing
of you   faithful woman
beside me.

After all these years
knowing you   friend
shape-shift
folding to you   lover.

Heartsong heralds
lesbian bright morning
this certainty
still a surprise.

November 2006

I Believe in Miracles

eight years of relationship
seventeen years of friendship
friends become lovers
where are you from
separate entities yet
living together
tiny
cottage
urban
high
street
double
yellow
lines
no
parking
farmers'
market
love it
this dwelling
secret courtyard
wide walkway
trellis arch then
huge garden urban surprise
open space once farm land
ring of oaks beech willow
fertile earth empty grassed
nearby waters rushing millrace
view of hills waiting for us —
to paint flowers trees fruit
vegetables shrubs salads herbs
on this blank canvas
home at last.

Winter 2006-7

Index of first lines

PS AVALON PUBLISHING

About PS Avalon

PS Avalon Publishing is an independent and committed publisher offering a complete publishing service, including editorial, manuscript preparation, printing, promotion, marketing and distribution. As a small publisher enabled to take full advantage of the latest technological advances, PS Avalon Publishing can offer an alternative route for aspiring authors working in our particular fields of interest.

As well as publishing, we offer a comprehensive education programme including courses, seminars, group retreats, and other opportunities for personal and spiritual growth. Whilst the nature of our work means we engage with people from all around the world, we are based in Glastonbury which is in the West Country of England.

new poetry books

Our purpose is to bring you the best new poetry with a psychospiritual content. Our intent is to make poetry relevant to life, offering work that is contemplative and inspirational, with a dark, challenging edge.

self development books

We publish inspiring reading material aimed at enhancing your life development without overburdening you with too many words. Everything is kept as simple and as accessible as possible.

journals

With its full colour design, easy on-line availability, and most of all with its exciting and inspiring contents, *The Synthesist* journal is a popular offering to the psychospiritual world and beyond.

PS AVALON PUBLISHING
Box 1865, Glastonbury,
Somerset BA6 8YR, U.K.

www.psavalon.com

info@psavalon.com

ꞌn the United Kingdom
ꞌng Source UK Ltd.
ᴊ0001B/19-66/A